CW00555611

LOBBY DESIGN

daab

The lobby as an architectural and spatial concept which for some people, given its relatively recent importance, can seem rather ambiguous, and at times may be confused with the lounge. However the lounge is principally a place for relaxation, whereas the lobby can offer different possibilities over and above its principal function, which is giving access connecting the exterior with the interior of a building. Lobbies are spaces which are housed in public buildings and whose design and scope are ever more important, given the need to transmit well-being to the visitor, whether the building be offices, an airport, a hospital or purely an administrative area.

From a social and architectural viewpoint, the essential element today of a lobby is its use as intermediary between two environments and all that that entails. In other words, it serves as a reception area and is the first point of contact with the place visited from the street, an urban oasis which we leave to reach the interior and from where one can get one's bearings.

The complexity of the lobby enables it to include other functions apart from its own. It may house rest areas in the style of a lounge, or it could serve as a waiting room, or as a meeting place, where relationships are established, albeit momentarily. Thus, the lobby strives to reflect everything related to the functions of the building in a true and positive manner.

As a further aspect of communication with passers-by, it is the area of the building which is seen from the outside and which informs about the space we cannot see. Thus, it must be inviting and appeal to the onlooker.

To sum up, the lobby is a passing place, a transitory space. However, the great challenge for the architect and client is to achieve a space in which the visitor would like to stay.

Die *Lobby* als räumliches und architektonisches Konzept ist für manche eine etwas undefinierbare Idee, die oft mit *Lounge* verwechselt wird, vielleicht aufgrund der Tatsache, dass das Konzept *Lobby* erst in den letzten Jahren an Bedeutung gewonnen hat. Eine Lounge dient vor allem als Ruhezone, während die *Lobby* neben ihrer Hauptfunktion, nämlich als Eingangsbereich zu dienen, auch die Aufgabe übernehmen kann, das Äußere mit dem Inneren eines Gebäudes zu verbinden.

Lobbies sind Räume, die wir in öffentlichen Gebäuden finden, und deren Gestaltung und Planung jeden Tag an Bedeutung gewinnt. Man versucht, bei dem Besucher ein positives Gefühl für das Gebäude zu wecken, er soll sich wohl fühlen, egal, ob es sich um Büroräume, einen Flughafen, ein Krankenhaus oder ein reines Verwaltungsgebäude handelt.

Was unter sozialen und architektonischen Gesichtspunkten heutzutage aus einer *Lobby* ein grundlegendes Element macht, ist deren Funktion als Vermittler zwischen zwei Umgebungen. Das führt dazu, dass sie zum Vorzimmer wird, in dem der erste Kontakt mit dem Ort aufgenommen wird, den man von der Straße aus betreten hat. Eine städtische Oase, von der aus wir das Innere eines Gebäudes betreten und uns orientieren.

In dieser ganzen interessanten Komplexität kann eine *Lobby* auch andere Funktionen als ihre eigene im engsten Sinne erfüllen. So kann es Ruhebereiche in Art einer *Lounge* geben, oder sie kann als Wartesaal oder Ort, an dem man sich trifft oder verabschiedet, dienen, oder an dem man Beziehungen knüpft, auch wenn es sich dabei nur um flüchtige handelt. Sie muss also auf eine reale und positive Art und Weise all das vermitteln, was sich auf die Funktionen des Gebäudes bezieht.

Schließlich dient sie auch als Medium zur Kommunikation mit den Vorübergehenden, denn die *Lobby* ist der Teil eines Gebäudes, den man von außen sehen kann und der somit auch Information über die Innenräume vermittelt, die man von außen nicht sehen kann. Es sollte ein Raum sein, den man gerne betritt oder betrachtet.

Eine *Lobby* ist also definitiv ein Durchgangsraum, in dem man sich nur vorübergehend aufhält, und trotzdem stellt die Planung dieses Raumes eine große Herausforderung sowohl an den Architekten als auch an den Kunden dar. Ziel ist es, einen Raum zu gestalten, in dem der Besucher gerne bleiben würde.

Es posible que el *lobby*, como concepto espacial y arquitectónico, sea para algunos –a causa de la importancia que se le viene otorgando desde hace unos años– una idea algo indefinida, que en ocasiones se confunde con el concepto de *lounge*. Sin embargo, mientras que este último es principalmente una zona de descanso, el *lobby* engloba diferentes posibilidades dentro de su función básica, que es la de dar acceso y conectar el exterior con el interior del edificio.

Los *lobbies* son espacios que normalmente se ubican en los edificios públicos, y cuyo diseño y proyección adquieren día a día una mayor importancia debido a la necesidad de transmitir al visitante una sensación acogedora, que está estrechamente ligada al edificio que se visita, ya sean oficinas, aeropuertos, hospitales o edificios administrativos.

Lo que convierte al *lobby* en un elemento esencial desde el punto de vista social y arquitectónico es su función de intermediario entre dos entornos; es, así pues, la antesala, el primer contacto que el visitante tiene con el lugar al que accede desde la calle. Un oasis urbano en el que debe detenerse para acceder al interior y que le permite orientarse.

Gracias a su interesante complejidad, el *lobby* puede abarcar otras funciones aparte de la suya propia: puede incluir áreas de descanso, a modo de *lounge*, servir de sala de espera o ser un punto de encuentro y de despedida, en el que se establecen relaciones, aunque sean momentáneas. En este sentido, debe transmitir de forma real y positiva todo lo relacionado con las funciones del edificio.

Finalmente el *lobby*, como una forma más de comunicación con los transeúntes, es la parte del edificio que se percibe desde el exterior y, por tanto, dice mucho sobre el espacio que no se puede ver desde fuera en su totalidad. Para quien lo concibe debe ser, pues, un lugar al que el transeúnte desee acceder o que produzca placer contemplar. En definitiva, el *lobby* es un lugar de paso, un espacio transitorio; no obstante, el gran desafío, tanto para el arquitecto como para el cliente, es que se convierta en un espacio en el que el visitante desee quedarse.

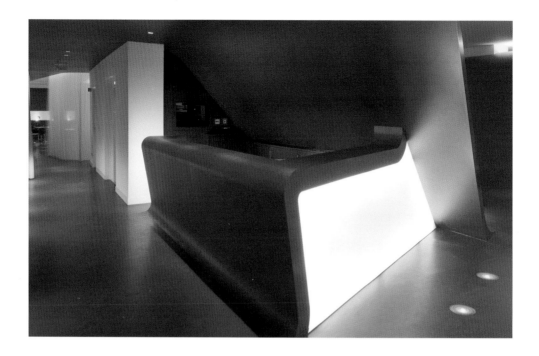

Le *lobby* en tant que concept spatial et architectural est pour certains, peut être en raison de l'importance relativement nouvelle qui lui est conférée depuis quelques années, une idée quelque peu indéfinie qui se confond parfois avec le *lounge*. Pour autant, alors que ce dernier revêt par essence une fonction de repos, le *lobby* peut recouvrir des possibilités distinctes au sein de sa fonction primordiale, celle d'offrir un accès, de connecter l'extérieur et l'intérieur d'un édifice.

Les lobbies sont des espaces que nous rencontrons dans les édifices destinés au public et dont le design et la projection acquièrent chaque jour davantage d'importance en raison du besoin de transmettre au visiteur un bien être lié à l'édifice visité, qu'il s'agisse de bureaux, d'un aéroport, d'un hôpital ou d'un immeuble purement administratif.

Ce qui offre son caractère essentiel au *lobby* d'un point de vue social et architectural, c'est sa fonction d'intermédiaire entre deux environnements et tout ce qu'elle implique : il sert d'antichambre et propose le premier contact avec le lieu auquel nous accédons depuis la rue. Une oasis urbaine s'offrant en point de départ pour accéder à l'intérieur et selon laquelle nous nous orientons.

Dans son intéressante complexité, le *lobby* peut couvrir d'autres fonctions outre la sienne propre et compter des aires de repos, sous forme de *lounge*, voire servant de salle d'attente ou de point de rencontre et de séparation où les relations naissent bien qu'elles restent uniquement momentanées. En ce sens, il doit transmettre de manière réelle et positive le corpus des fonctions de l'édifice.

Finalement, un autre aspect de la communication avec les passants, le *lobby* est la partie de l'édifice qui est perçue depuis l'extérieur et qui en dit long sur l'espace qui demeure invisible de l'extérieur. Pour son créateur, ce doit être un lieu auquel l'on souhaite accéder ou suscitant un plaisir contemplatif.

En définitive, le *lobby* est un lieu de passage, un espace transitoire. Cependant, le grand défi, en tant que centre d'intérêt de l'architecte et de son client, est de réussir un espace au sein duquel le visiteur souhaite rester.

Il *lobby* come concetto spaziale ed architettonico è per alcuni, forse per l'importanza relativamente nuova che gli viene data da qualche anno, un'idea poco definita, che a volte si confonde con il *lounge*. Ma, mentre il *lounge* ha una funzione principalmente di riposo, il *lobby* può implicare varie possibilità in seno alla sua primordiale funzione di dare accesso e collegare l'esterno con l'interno dell'edificio.

I *lobby* sono degli spazi che si trovano negli edifici d'uso pubblico con un disegno e una proiezione che acquisiscono un'importanza sempre più rilevante per la necessità di trasmettere al visitatore un benessere relativo all'edificio che si visita, siano essi uffici, un aeroporto, un ospedale o un edificio puramente amministrativo.

Quello che dal punto di vista sociale ed architettonico rende, oggigiorno, il *lobby* un elemento essenziale è la sua funzione di intermediario tra due ambienti e tutto quello che ciò comporta; ovvero, funge da antisala, è il primo contatto con il luogo a cui si accede dalla strada. Un'oasi urbana dalla quale si parte per accedere all'interno che serve ad orientarsi.

In tutta la sua interessante complessità, il *lobby* può comprendere altre funzioni oltre la sua, e contare con zone di riposo, a modo di *lounge*, oppure fungendo da sala d'attesa, o come luogo d'incontro e di commiato in cui si instaurano relazioni, benché solo momentanee. In tal senso, deve trasmettere in modo reale e positivo tutto quello che è in relazione con le funzioni dell'edificio.

Infine, come un aspetto in più della comunicazione con i passanti, il *lobby* è l'area dell'edificio che s'intravede dall'esterno e dice molto sul suo spazio che non si può vedere dal di fuori. Per chi lo concepisce, deve essere un luogo in cui si abbia voglia di accedere o che faccia piacere contemplare.

In definitiva, il *lobby* è un luogo di passaggio, uno spazio transitorio; sebbene la grande sfida, come nucleo d'interesse per l'architetto e per il suo cliente, sia quella di riuscire a fare in modo di renderlo uno spazio in cui il visitatore voglia restare.

ACQ ARCHITECTS | LONDON
SPARK AND EO OFFICES
London, UK | 2003

BARKOW LEIBINGER ARCHITEKTEN | BERLIN
VERTRIEBS-UND SERVICEZENTRUM
Stuttgart, Germany | 2003

BLAINEY NORTH & ASSOCIATES | SYDNEY
HAWKER PACIFIC FLIGHT CENTRE
Sydney, Australia | 2004

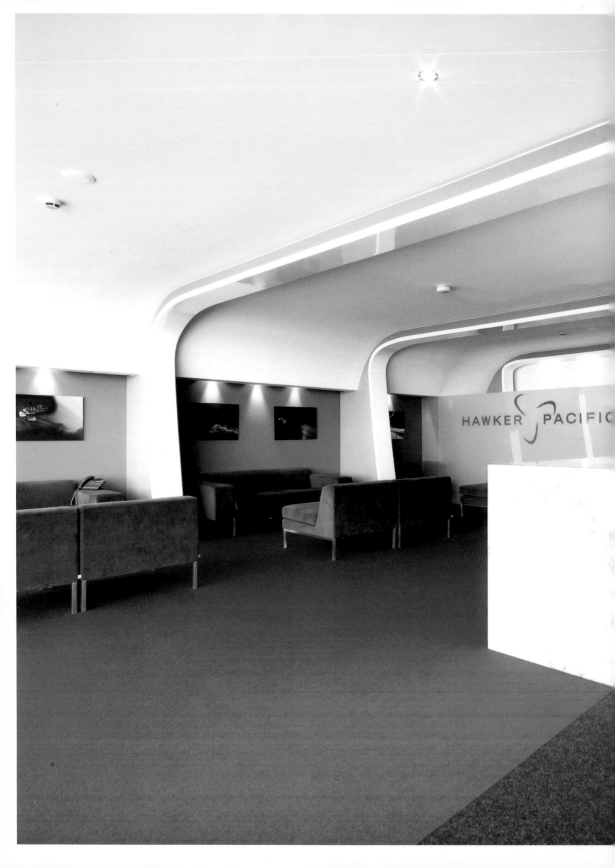

BOLLES & WILSON | MÜNSTER
NEW LUXOR THEATRE
Rotterdam, Netherlands | 2001

BOLLES & WILSON | MÜNSTER
STAFF LOBBY
Lemgo, Germany | 1999

CHRISTIAN DE PORTZAMPARC ATELIER | PARIS
PHILARMONIE DE LUXEMBOURG
Luxembourg, Luxembourg | 2005

CHRISTIAN WERNER | HOLLENSTEDT, APPEL
ROLF BENZ MESSE
Cologne, Germany | 2004

CONCRETE ARCHITECTURAL ASSOCIATES | AMSTERDAM
ÜBERFLUSS HOTEL
Bremen, Germany | 2005

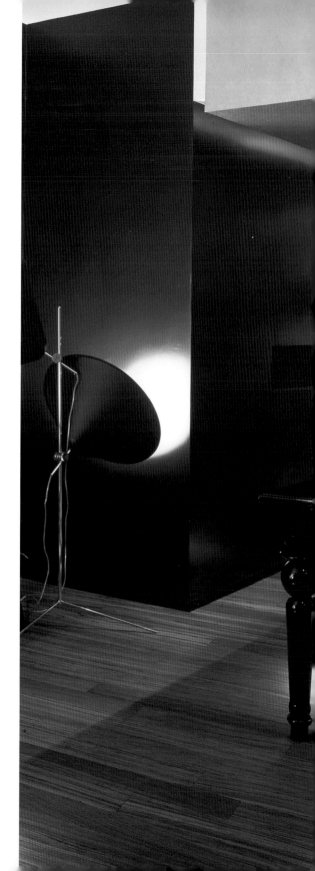

CONCRETE ARCHITECTURAL ASSOCIATES | AMSTERDAM
VAN GOGH MUSEUM
Amsterdam, Netherlands | 2000

CONRAN & PARTNERS | LONDON
HOTEL PARK NEW DELHI
New Delhi, India | 1997

DAM & PARTNERS ARCHITECTEN | AMSTERDAM
KLUWER OFFICE BUILDING
Alphen Aan Den Rijn, Netherlands | 2003

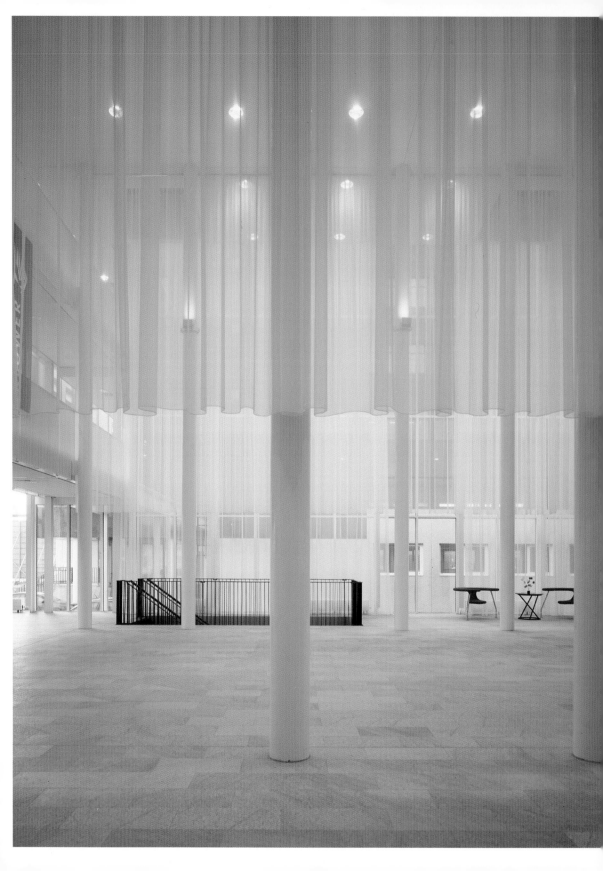

DENNISTON | KUALA LUMPUR
THE CHEDI MUSCAT
Muscat, Oman | 2004

(aus: Franz Kafka, Einleitungsvortrag über
Rezitationsabend des jiddischen Schauspie

DIETRICH & UNTERTRIFALLER ARCHITEKTEN | BREGENZ
VIENNA THEATER
Vienna, Austria | 2006

(aus: Franz Kafka, Einleitungsvortrag über Jargon, gehalten am 18. 02. 1912 vor einem
Rezitationsabend des jiddischen Schauspielers Jizchak Löwy in Prag)

DREWES & STRENGE ARCHITEKTEN | HERZEBROCK-CLARHOLZ
BERTELSMANN LOBBY
Versmold, Germany | 2002

ERICK VAN EGERAAT ASSOCIATED ARCHITECTS | ROTTERDAM
CITY HALL
Alpen Aan Den Rijn, Netherlands | 2002

ESPINET UBACH ARQUITECTES ASSOCIATS | BARCELONA
CITY HALL
Salou, Spain | 2005

ESPINET UBACH ARQUITECTES ASSOCIATS | BARCELONA
HOTEL RA
El Vendrell, Spain | 2004

FRANCESC RIFÉ | BARCELONA
CAVES EL CEP
Sant Sadurní d'Anoia, Spain | 2003

RESPECTANT SÁVIAMENT LA
TRADICIÓ I ELS CONEIXEMENTS
ACUMULATS AL LLARG DE
GENERACIONS, SABEDORS
DE LA SITUACIÓ PRIVILEGIADA
DE LES NOSTRES VINYES I DE
L'ART D'ELABORAR VI, I OBERTS
A LES NOVES TECNOLOGIES I
INNOVACIONS, ACONSEGUIM
ELS NOSTRES VINS I CAVES DE
PERSONALITAT DIFERENCIADA
ARREU DEL MÓN.

GABELLINI SHEPPARD ASSOCIATES | NEW YORK
ROCKEFELLER CENTER
New York, USA | 2005

GCA ARQUITECTES | BARCELONA
CENTRE D'ARTESANIA DE CATALUNYA
Barcelona, Spain | 2004

GCA ARQUITECTES | BARCELONA
CRAM L'HOTEL
Barcelona, Spain | 2004

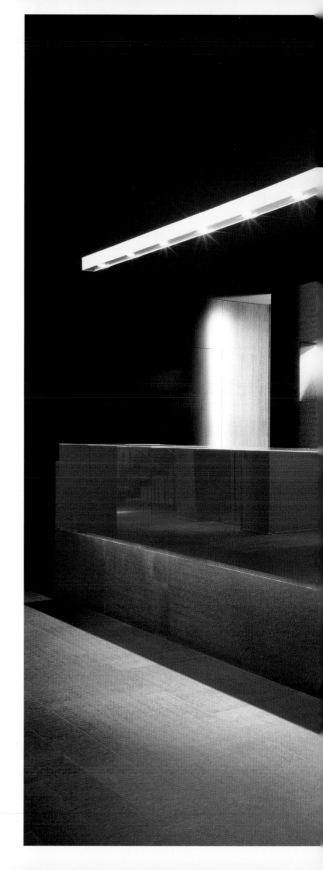

GCA ARQUITECTES | BARCELONA
HOTEL PRESTIGE
Barcelona, Spain | 2002

GOHM & HIESSBERGER ARCHITEKTURBÜRO | FELDKIRCH
HOSPITAL DORNBIRN
Dornbirn, Austria | 2006

GRAFT GESELLSCHAFT VON ARCHITEKTEN | BERLIN
HOTEL Q
Berlin, Germany | 2004

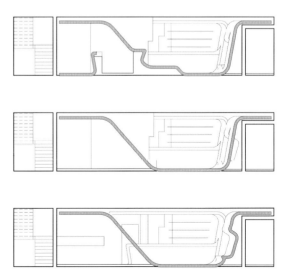

GRAFT GESELLSCHAFT VON ARCHITEKTEN | BERLIN
KU64
Berlin, Germany | 2004

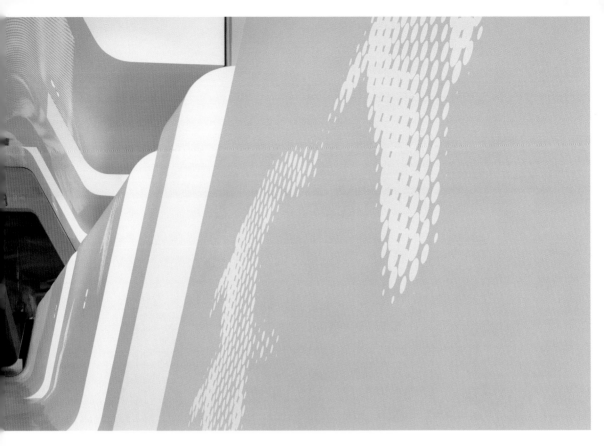

GRAY PUKSAND ARCHITECTS | SYDNEY
441 OFFICE
Melbourne, Australia | 2005

GRAY PUKSAND ARCHITECTS | SYDNEY
OFFICE IN MELBOURNE
Melbourne, Australia | 2004

JANE FOLEY | SYDNEY
BATES SMART OFFICES
Sydney, Australia | 2003

JEAN NOUVEL ATELIER | PARIS
THE HOTEL
Lucerne, Switzerland | 2000

JOSEP LLUÍS MATEO - MAP ARCHITECTS | BARCELONA
HOTEL AC FORUM
Barcelona, Spain | 2004

JOSEP M. FARGAS | BARCELONA
TORRE FARGAS
Barcelona, Spain

KOHN PEDERSEN FOX ASSOCIATES | LONDON
BENRATHER KARREE
Düsseldorf, Germany | 2002

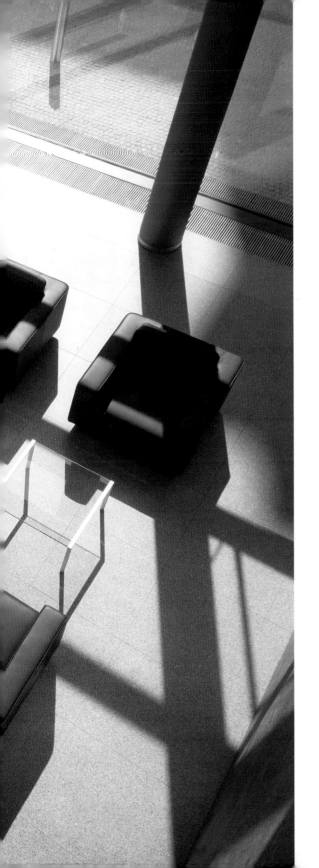

KPMB ARCHITECTS | TORONTO
CENTENNIAL HP SCIENCE AND TECHNOLOGY CENTRE
Scarborough, Canada | 2004

KPMB ARCHITECTS | TORONTO
JAMES STEWART CENTRE FOR MATHEMATICS
Hamilton, Canada | 2003

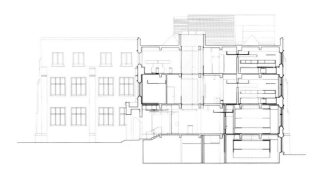

LANDAU & KINDELBACHER | MUNICH
KANGAROOS
Pirmasens, Germany | 2005

LANDOR ASSOCIATES | LONDON
AUSTRIAN AIRLINES
Vienna, Austria | 2003

MARTÍN RUIZ DE AZÚA | BARCELONA
RADIO BARCELONA
Barcelona, Spain | 2004

MASSIMO MARIANI | MONTECATINI TERME
BANCO DI CREDITO COOPERATIVO DI CASTAGNETO CARDUCCI
Castagneto Carducci, Italy | 2002

MICHAEL STROBL | SALZBURG
WÜSTENROT HEADQUARTER
Salzburg, Austria | 2005

NIALL D. BRENNAN, HELEN KILMARTIN | DUBLIN
THE MORGAN HOTEL
Dublin, Ireland | 1997

NURMELA, RAIMORANTA, TASA | HELSINKI
UNIVERSITY OF TURKU
Turku, Finland | 2003

ROGER BELLERA | GIRONA
LOOP TELECOM OFFICES
Barcelona, Spain | 2001

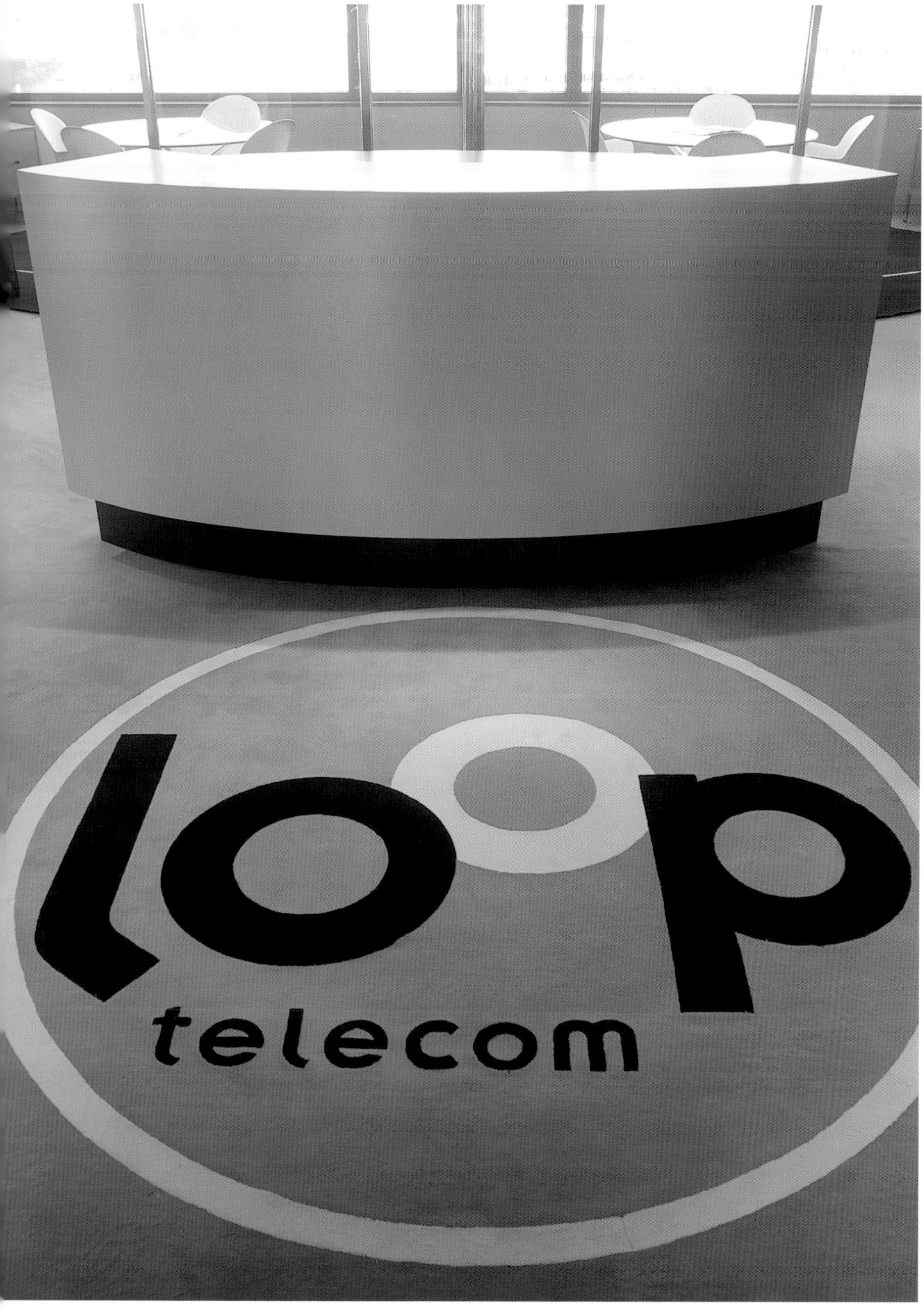
loop
telecom

ROLF LÖFVENBERG, LARS PIHL, JAN SÖDER | STOCKHOLM
NORDIC LIGHT HOTEL
Stockholm, Sweden | 2001

SABINE MESCHEROWSKY | KREFELD
HOTEL MADLEIN
Ischgl, Austria | 2004

SANDELL SANDBERG | STOCKHOLM
CATELLA CAPITAL
Stockholm, Sweden | 2006

SATIJN PLUS ARCHITECTEN | BORN
KRUISHEREN KLOSTER HOTEL
Maastricht, The Netherlands | 2005

SCHARNBERGER ARCHITEKTEN, OANA ROSEN | FRANKFURT
THE PURE HOTEL
Frankfurt, Germany | 2005

SKIDMORE, OWINGS & MERRILL | CHICAGO
CANARY WHARF, DS1 BUILDING
London, UK | 2005

SPECTER DESOUZA ARCHITECTS | NEW YORK
80 PINE STREET
New York, USA | 2005

SPECTER DESOUZA ARCHITECTS | NEW YORK
485 MADISON STREET
New York, USA | 2002

STAAB ARCHITEKTEN | BERLIN
INSTITUT FÜR GENOMFORSCHUNG
Berlin, Germany | 2005

STUDIO GAIA | NEW YORK
W HOTEL SEOUL
Seoul, South Korea | 2005

STUDIO IOSA GHINI | BOLOGNA
AUTO SALONI MIAMI
Miami, USA | 2004

WESTFOURTH ARCHITECTURE | NEW YORK
CDG CENTER
Bucharest, Romania | 2005

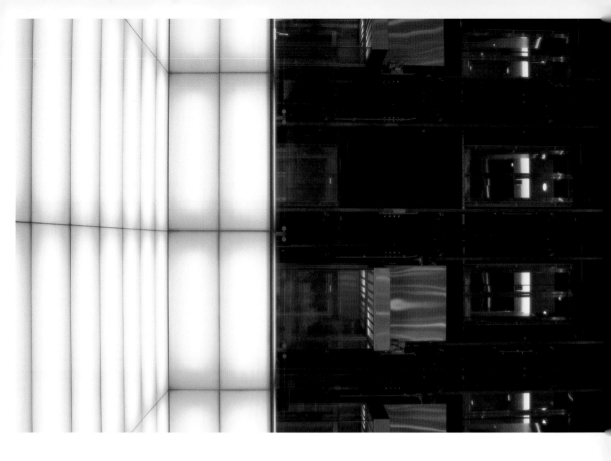

ZIPHER SPACEWORKS | STUTTGART
PANAMA WERBEAGENTUR
Stuttgart, Germany | 2001

zustimmen

ACQ Architects
4 John Prince's Street
London W1G OJL, UK
P +44 0 20 7491 4272
F +44 0 20 7491 4854
www.acq-architects.com
Spark and EO Offices
Photos: © Richard Davies

Barkow Leibinger Architekten
Schillerstrasse 94
10625 Berlin, Germany
P +49 0 3031 5712 0
F +49 0 3031 5712 29
www.barkowleibinger.com
Vertriebs-und Servicezentrum
Photos: © Margherita Spiluttini
         © David Franck

Blainey North & Associates Pty. Ltd.
38 Kings Lane, Republic One
East Sydney, NSW 2010, Australia
P +61 02 9358 4866
F +61 02 9475 1266
www.blaineynorth.com
Hawker Pacific Flight Centre
Photos: © Steve Back

Bolles & Wilson GmbH & Co. KG
Hafenweg 16
48155 Münster, Germany
P +49 2514 8272 0
F +49 2514 8272 24
www.bolles-wilson.com
New Luxor Theatre
Staff Lobby
Photos: © Christian Richters

Christian de Portzamparc Atelier
1 Rue de l'Aude
75014 Paris, France
P +33 1 40 64 80 00
F +33 1 43 27 74 79
www.chdeportzamparc.com
Philarmonie de Luxembourg
Photos: © Christian Richters

Christian Werner
Am Aarbach 14
21279 Hollenstedt, Appel, Germany
P +49 4165 2126 12
F +49 4165 2126 13
www.christian-werner.com
Rolf Benz Messe
Photos: © H.-G. Esch

Cibic & Partners
Via Varese 18
20121 Milano, Italy
P +39 02 65 71122
F +39 02 29 060141
www.cibicpartners.com
I net British Telecom
Photos: © Santi Caleca

Concrete Architectural Associates
Rozengracht 133 III
1016 LV Amsterdam, The Netherlands
P +31 0 20 520 0200
F +31 0 20 520 0201
www.concreteamsterdam.nl
Überfluss Hotel
Van Gogh Museum
Photos: © Luuk Kramer

Conran & Partners
22 Shad Thames
London SEI 2YU, UK
P +44 20 7403 8899
F +44 20 7357 0832
www.conranandpartners.com
Hotel Park New Delhi
Photos: © Design Hotels

Dam & Partners Architecten
Schipluidenlaan 4
1062 HE Amsterdam, The Netherlands
P +31 20 623 4755
F +31 20 627 7280
www.damenpartners.com
Kluwer Office Building
Photos: © Luuk Kramer

Denniston Sdn. Bhd.
UBN Tower, 26th Floor
10, Jalan P. Ramlee
50250 Kuala Lumpur, Malaysia
P +60 603 2031 3418
F +60 603 2031 3422
www.denniston.com.my
The Chedi Muscat
Photos: © Design Hotels

Dietrich & Untertrifaller Architekten
Arlberggasse 117
6900 Bregenz, Austria
P +43 5574 78888 0
F +43 5574 78888 20
www.dietrich.untertrifaller.com
Vienna Theater
Photos: © Bruno Klomfar

Drewes & Strenge Architekten
Bahnhofstrasse 10 a
33442 Herzebrock-Clarholz, Germany
P +49 5245 3208
F +49 5245 1871 0
www.drewesstrenge.com
Bertelsmann Lobby
Photos: © Christian Richters

Eric van Egeraat Associated Architects
Calanderstraat 23
3016 CA Rotterdam, The Netherlands
P +31 0 10 436 9686
F +31 0 10 436 9773
www.eea-architects.com
City Hall
Photos: © Christian Richters

Espinet Ubach Arquitectes Associats
Camp 63
08023 Barcelona, Spain
P +34 934 187 833
F +34 934 172 122
espinet-ubach@retemail.es
City Hall
Hotel Ra
Photos © Lluís Casals

Francesc Rifé
Escoles Pies 25
08017 Barcelona, Spain
P +34 934 141 288
F +34 932 412 814
www.rife-design.com
Caves El Cep
Photos: © Eugeni Pons

Gabellini Sheppard Associates LLP
665 Broadway Suite 706
New York, NY 10012, USA
P + 1 212 388 1700
F + 1 212 388 1808
www.gabelliniassociates.com
Rockefeller Center
Photos: © Paul Warchol

GCA Arquitectes
Calle Valencia 289
08009 Barcelona, Spain
P +34 934 761 800
www.gcaarq.com
Centre d'Artesania de Catalunya
Cram L'Hotel
Hotel Prestige
Photos: © Jordi Miralles

Gohm & Hiessberger Architekturbüro
Montfortgasse 1
6800 Feldkirch, Austria
P +43 5522 32801
F +43 5522 32801 8
www.gohmhiessberger.com
Hospital Dornbirn
Photos: © Bruno Klomfar

Graft Gesellschaft von Architekten mbH
Borsigstrasse 33
10115 Berlin, Germany
P +49 30 2404 7985
F +49 30 2404 7987
www.graftlab.com
Hotel Q
KU64
Photos: © Hiepler, Brunier

Gray Puksand Architects
Level 5, 8 Spring Street
Sydney NSW 2000, Australia
P +61 02 9247 9422
F +61 02 9247 9433
www.graypuksand.com.au
441 Office
Office in Melbourne
Photos: © Shania Shegedyn

Helen Kilmartin (interior designer)
8 Herbert place
Dublin 2, Ireland
P + 353 1 662 7894
F + 353 1 662 7896
www.minima.ie
The Morgan Hotel
Photos: © Design Hotels

Jane Foley
Sydney, Australia
Bates Smart Offices
Photos: © Murray Fredericks

Jean Nouvel Atelier
10 Cité d'Angoulême
75011 Paris, France
P +33 1 49 23 83 83
F +33 1 43 14 81 10
www.jeannouvel.com
The Hotel
Photos: © Design Hotels

Josep Lluís Mateo - MAP Architects
Teodor Roviralta 39
08022 Barcelona, Spain
P +34 932 186 358
F +34 932 185 292
www.mateo-maparchitect.com
Hotel AC Forum
Photos: © Jordi Miralles

Josep M. Fargas
Muntaner 477
08021 Barcelona, Spain
P +34 934 179 007
F +34 934 176 805
www.fargas.net
Torre Fargas
Photos: © Jordi Miralles

Kohn Pedersen Fox Associates
13 Langley Street
London WC2H 9JG, UK
P +44 0 20 7596 4334
F +44 0 20 7497 1175
www.kpf.com
Benrather Karree
Photos: © H.-G. Esch

KPMB Architects
322 King Street West, Third Floor
Toronto, Ontario M5V 1J2, Canada
P +1 416 977 5104
F +1 416 598 9840
www.kpmbarchitects.com
Centennial HP Science and Technology Centre
James Stewart Centre for Mathematics
Photos: © Tom Arban Photography

Landau & Kindelbacher
Tattenbachstrasse 18
80538 Munich, Germany
P +49 89 24 2289 0
F +49 89 24 2289 24
www.landaukindelbacher.com
KangaROOS
Photos: © Florian Holzherr

Landor Associates/London headquarters
Klamath House, 18 Clerkenwell Green
London EC1R ODP, UK
P +44 207 880 8000
F +44 207 800 8801
www.landor.com
Austrian Airlines
Photos: © Carlos Dominguez

Lars Pihl, Jan Söder
Vasaplan 7
10137 Stockholm, Sweden
P +46 8 50 56 32 55/57
Nordic Light Hotel
Photos: © Design Hotels

Martín Ruiz de Azúa
Rambla del Prat 8, 2.º 2.ª
08012 Barcelona, Spain
P/F +34 932 182 914
www.martinazua.com
Radio Barcelona
Photos: © Jordi Miralles

Massimo Mariani
Via Don Minzoni 27
Montecatini Terme, PT, Italy
P +39 0572 766324
F +39 0572 912742
www.massimomariani.net
Banco di Credito Cooperativo
Photos: © Alessandro Ciampi

Michael Strobl
Rottmayrgasse 23
5020 Salzburg, Austria
P +43 6628 72108
F +43 6628 72366
www.michaelstrobl.at
Wüstenrot Headquarter
Photos: © J. Unterhauser, P. Schafleitner

Niall D. Brennan Associates
24 Fitzwilliam place
Dublin 2, Ireland
P +353 1 678 9955
F +353 1 661 6347
www.ndba.ie
The Morgan Hotel
Photos: © Design Hotels

Nurmela, Raimoranta, Tasa
Kalevankatu 31
00100 Helsinki, Finland
www.n-r-t.fi
University of Turku
Photos: © Antti Luutonen

Oana Rosen
Westendstrasse 46
60325 Frankfurt, Germany
T +49 177 888 5999
The Pure Hotel
Photos: © Design Hotels

Roger Bellera
Produccions de Disseny Bellera s.l.
Pça. de l´Esglèsia, s/n Galeries Begur
17255 Begur-Girona, Spain
P +34 629 783 112
roger@produccionsbellera.com
Loop Telecom Offices
Photos: © Jordi Miralles

Rolf Löfvenberg AB/Hotell och.
Restaurangprojektering
Skeppar Karls gränd 4
11130 Stockholm, Sweden
P +46 8 24 34 75
Nordic Light Hotel
Photos: © Design Hotels

Sabine Mescherowsky
Oelschlägerstr. 65
47798 Krefeld, Germany
Hotel Madlein
Photos: © Design Hotels

Sandell Sandberg
Linnégatan 89E
115 23 Stockholm, Sweden
P +46 0 8 50653122
F +46 0 8 50621707
www.sandellsandberg.se
Catella Capital
Photos: ©Johan Oedmann

Satijn Plus Architecten
Postbus 210
6120 Ba Born, Kasteelhof 1
6121 xk Born, The Netherlands
P +31 0 46 420 5555
F +31 0 46 420 5566
www.satijnplus.nl
Kruisheren Kloster Hotel
Photos: © Design Hotels

Scharnberger Architekten
Lenaustrasse 80
60318 Frankfurt, Germany
P +49 69 555 776
www.scharnberger.de
The Pure Hotel
Photos: © Design Hotels

Skidmore, Owings & Merrill LLP
224 S. Michigan Avenue, Suite 1000
Chicago IL 60604, USA
P +1 312 554 9090
F +1 312 360 4545
www.som.com
Canary Wharf, DS1 Building
Photos: © H.-G. Esch

Specter DeSouza Architects PC
2061 Broadway
New York NY 10023, USA
P +1 212 724 6600
F +1 212 724 6673
www.specterdesouza.com
80 Pine Street
485 Madison Street
Photos: © Elliot Kaufman Photography

Staab Architekten BDA
Schlesische Strasse 20
10997 Berlin, Germany
P +49 3061 7914 20
F +49 3061 7914 11
www.staab-architekten.com
Institut für Genomforschung
Photos: © Stefan Meyer

Studio Gaia
401 Washington Street, 4th Floor
New York NY 10013, USA
P +1 212 680 3500
F +1 212 680 3535
www.studiogaia.com
W Hotel Seoul
Photos: © Seung Hoon, Youn Kim

Studio Iosa Ghini
Via Castiglione 6
40124 Bologna, Italy
P +39 051 236563
F +39 051 237712
www.iosaghini.it
Auto Saloni Miami
Photos: © santi Caleca

Westfourth Architecture PC
632 Broadway, Suite 801
New York, NY 10012, USA
P +1 212 388 9227
F +1 212 388 9228
www.westfourth-architecture.com
CDG Center
Photos: © Mihail Moldoveanu

Zipher Spaceworks
Bismarckstrasse 67 B
70197 Stuttgart, Germany
P +49 711 99 33 92 330
F +49 711 99 33 92 333
www.zipher.de
Panama Werbeagentur
Photos: © Zooey Braun

© 2006 daab
cologne london new york

published and distributed worldwide by
daab gmbh
friesenstr. 50
d - 50670 köln

p +49 - 221 - 913 927 0
f +49 - 221 - 913 927 20

mail@daab-online.com
www.daab-online.com

publisher ralf daab
rdaab@daab-online.com

creative director feyyaz
mail@feyyaz.com

editorial project by loft publications
© 2006 loft publications

editor and text montse borràs
research beate küper

layout oriol serra juncosa
english translation heather bagott
french translation michel ficerai
italian translation donatella talpo
german translation susanne engler

printed in spain
Anman Gràfiques del Vallès, Spain
www.anman.com

isbn-10   3 - 937718 - 57 - 5
isbn-13   978 - 3 - 937718 - 57 - 6
dl   B - 49701 - 06